This journal belongs to:

How to use this journal

The Food For Friends journal will ensure you are well equipped to host unforgettable gatherings. It features convenient sections to assist in planning for dinner parties or any occasions where you'll be cooking for guests.

Use the 'Party Plan' section to streamline your event preparation where, on a double page spread, you can list your guests, map out menus and compile shopping lists.

Keep track of your guests' food allergies or intolerances, and any special dietary requirements in the 'Guest Info' section. Additionally, there is a place to record what you've previously served them to avoid repetition. The 'Guest Log' includes space to note down the page number of each guest in the 'Guest Info' section for quick referencing.

In the 'Recipes' section, document your culinary adventures by noting down recipes you've tried, as well as those you plan to make in the future. The 'Recipe Log' includes space to note the recipe name and its corresponding page number to easily find in the future.

Finally, record stories and memorable anecdotes in the 'Reflections' section, a great place to capture memories of all your dinner party adventures.

Index

Party Plan 5

Guest Log 21

Guest Info 25

Recipe Log 63

Recipes 67

Kitchen Measurements 101

Reflections 107

Party Plan

Party Plan

Date: .... How many guests? ....

Guests

....   ☐ Allergies
....   ☐ Vegetarian
....   ☐ Vegan
....   ☐ Gluten Free
....   ☐ Dairy Free

Starter

Main

Dessert

Drinks

Shopping List

Party Plan

Date: .... How many guests? ....

Guests

.... ☐ Allergies
.... ☐ Vegetarian
.... ☐ Vegan
.... ☐ Gluten Free
.... ☐ Dairy Free

Starter

Main

Dessert

Drinks

Shopping List

Party Plan

Date: .... How many guests? ....

Guests

.... ☐ Allergies
.... ☐ Vegetarian
.... ☐ Vegan
.... ☐ Gluten Free
.... ☐ Dairy Free

Starter

Main

Dessert

Drinks

Shopping List

Party Plan

Date: .... How many guests? ....

Guests

....	....	☐ Allergies
....	....	☐ Vegetarian
....	....	☐ Vegan
....	....	☐ Gluten Free
....	....	☐ Dairy Free

Starter

Main

Dessert

Drinks

Shopping List

Party Plan

Date: .... How many guests? ....

Guests

....	....	☐ Allergies
....	....	☐ Vegetarian
....	....	☐ Vegan
....	....	☐ Gluten Free
....	....	☐ Dairy Free

Starter

Main

Dessert

Drinks

Shopping List

Party Plan

Date: .... How many guests? ....

Guests

....	....	☐ Allergies
....	....	☐ Vegetarian
....	....	☐ Vegan
....	....	☐ Gluten Free
....	....	☐ Dairy Free

Starter

Main

Dessert

Drinks

Shopping List

Party Plan

Date: .... How many guests? ....

Guests

....	....	☐ Allergies
....	....	☐ Vegetarian
....	....	☐ Vegan
....	....	☐ Gluten Free
....	....	☐ Dairy Free

Starter

Main

Dessert

Drinks

Shopping List

Guest Log

Guest Log . . .

Name	Page

Name	Page

Guest Info

Guest Name:

Dietary Requirements

☐ Allergies
☐ Vegetarian
☐ Vegan
☐ Gluten Free
☐ Dairy Free

Likes

Dislikes

Date | Food Served

Guest Name:

Dietary Requirements

- [ ] Allergies
- [ ] Vegetarian
- [ ] Vegan
- [ ] Gluten Free
- [ ] Dairy Free

Likes

Dislikes

Date	Food Served

Guest Name: ....

Dietary Requirements

.... ☐ Allergies
.... ☐ Vegetarian
.... ☐ Vegan
.... ☐ Gluten Free
.... ☐ Dairy Free

Likes	Dislikes
....	....
....	....
....	....
....	....
....	....

Date	Food Served

Guest Name:

Dietary Requirements

☐ Allergies
☐ Vegetarian
☐ Vegan
☐ Gluten Free
☐ Dairy Free

Likes

Dislikes

Date	Food Served

Guest Name: ....

Dietary Requirements

.... ☐ Allergies
.... ☐ Vegetarian
.... ☐ Vegan
.... ☐ Gluten Free
.... ☐ Dairy Free

Likes

Dislikes

Date	Food Served

Guest Name:

Dietary Requirements

☐ Allergies
☐ Vegetarian
☐ Vegan
☐ Gluten Free
☐ Dairy Free

Likes

Dislikes

Date	Food Served

Guest Name: ....

Dietary Requirements

.... ☐ Allergies
.... ☐ Vegetarian
.... ☐ Vegan
.... ☐ Gluten Free
.... ☐ Dairy Free

Likes	Dislikes

Date	Food Served

Guest Name:

Dietary Requirements

☐ Allergies
☐ Vegetarian
☐ Vegan
☐ Gluten Free
☐ Dairy Free

Likes

Dislikes

Date | Food Served

Guest Name: ....

Dietary Requirements

.... ☐ Allergies
.... ☐ Vegetarian
.... ☐ Vegan
.... ☐ Gluten Free
.... ☐ Dairy Free

Likes	Dislikes
....	....
....	....
....	....
....	....
....	....

Date	Food Served

Guest Name:

Dietary Requirements

☐ Allergies
☐ Vegetarian
☐ Vegan
☐ Gluten Free
☐ Dairy Free

Likes

Dislikes

Date	Food Served

Guest Name:

Dietary Requirements

☐ Allergies
☐ Vegetarian
☐ Vegan
☐ Gluten Free
☐ Dairy Free

Likes

Dislikes

Date | Food Served

Guest Name:

Dietary Requirements

- [ ] Allergies
- [ ] Vegetarian
- [ ] Vegan
- [ ] Gluten Free
- [ ] Dairy Free

Likes

Dislikes

Date | Food Served

Guest Name:

Dietary Requirements

☐ Allergies
☐ Vegetarian
☐ Vegan
☐ Gluten Free
☐ Dairy Free

Likes

Dislikes

Date | Food Served

Guest Name: ....

Dietary Requirements

.... ☐ Allergies
.... ☐ Vegetarian
.... ☐ Vegan
.... ☐ Gluten Free
.... ☐ Dairy Free

Likes

Dislikes

Date — Food Served

Guest Name:

Dietary Requirements

☐ Allergies
☐ Vegetarian
☐ Vegan
☐ Gluten Free
☐ Dairy Free

Likes

Dislikes

Date	Food Served

Guest Name:

Dietary Requirements

- [ ] Allergies
- [ ] Vegetarian
- [ ] Vegan
- [ ] Gluten Free
- [ ] Dairy Free

Likes

Dislikes

Date	Food Served

Guest Name: ....

Dietary Requirements

.... ☐ Allergies
.... ☐ Vegetarian
.... ☐ Vegan
.... ☐ Gluten Free
.... ☐ Dairy Free

Likes | Dislikes

Date	Food Served

Guest Name:

Dietary Requirements

- [ ] Allergies
- [ ] Vegetarian
- [ ] Vegan
- [ ] Gluten Free
- [ ] Dairy Free

Likes

Dislikes

Date	Food Served

Guest Name:

Dietary Requirements

- [ ] Allergies
- [ ] Vegetarian
- [ ] Vegan
- [ ] Gluten Free
- [ ] Dairy Free

Likes

Dislikes

Date | Food Served

Guest Name:

Dietary Requirements

- [ ] Allergies
- [ ] Vegetarian
- [ ] Vegan
- [ ] Gluten Free
- [ ] Dairy Free

Likes

Dislikes

Date | Food Served

Guest Name: ....

Dietary Requirements

.... ☐ Allergies
.... ☐ Vegetarian
.... ☐ Vegan
.... ☐ Gluten Free
.... ☐ Dairy Free

Likes | Dislikes

Likes	Dislikes

Date | Food Served

Date	Food Served

Guest Name: ....

Dietary Requirements

.... ☐ Allergies
.... ☐ Vegetarian
.... ☐ Vegan
.... ☐ Gluten Free
.... ☐ Dairy Free

Likes	Dislikes

Date	Food Served

Guest Name: ....

Dietary Requirements

.... ☐ Allergies
.... ☐ Vegetarian
.... ☐ Vegan
.... ☐ Gluten Free
.... ☐ Dairy Free

Likes	Dislikes

Date	Food Served

Guest Name:

Dietary Requirements

☐ Allergies
☐ Vegetarian
☐ Vegan
☐ Gluten Free
☐ Dairy Free

Likes

Dislikes

Date	Food Served

Guest Name: ....

Dietary Requirements

.... ☐ Allergies
.... ☐ Vegetarian
.... ☐ Vegan
.... ☐ Gluten Free
.... ☐ Dairy Free

Likes	Dislikes

Date	Food Served

Guest Name: ....

Dietary Requirements

.... ☐ Allergies
.... ☐ Vegetarian
.... ☐ Vegan
.... ☐ Gluten Free
.... ☐ Dairy Free

Likes	Dislikes

Date	Food Served

Guest Name: ....

Dietary Requirements

.... ☐ Allergies
.... ☐ Vegetarian
.... ☐ Vegan
.... ☐ Gluten Free
.... ☐ Dairy Free

Likes	Dislikes

Date	Food Served

Guest Name: ....

Dietary Requirements

.... ☐ Allergies
.... ☐ Vegetarian
.... ☐ Vegan
.... ☐ Gluten Free
.... ☐ Dairy Free

Likes	Dislikes

Date	Food Served

Guest Name: ....

Dietary Requirements

- [ ] Allergies
- [ ] Vegetarian
- [ ] Vegan
- [ ] Gluten Free
- [ ] Dairy Free

Likes

Dislikes

Date	Food Served

Guest Name: ....

Dietary Requirements

.... ☐ Allergies
.... ☐ Vegetarian
.... ☐ Vegan
.... ☐ Gluten Free
.... ☐ Dairy Free

Likes	Dislikes

Date	Food Served

Guest Name: ....

Dietary Requirements

- [ ] Allergies
- [ ] Vegetarian
- [ ] Vegan
- [ ] Gluten Free
- [ ] Dairy Free

Likes

Dislikes

Date | Food Served

Guest Name:

Dietary Requirements

☐ Allergies
☐ Vegetarian
☐ Vegan
☐ Gluten Free
☐ Dairy Free

Likes

Dislikes

Date | Food Served

Guest Name:

Dietary Requirements

- [ ] Allergies
- [ ] Vegetarian
- [ ] Vegan
- [ ] Gluten Free
- [ ] Dairy Free

Likes

Dislikes

Date	Food Served

Guest Name:

Dietary Requirements

- [ ] Allergies
- [ ] Vegetarian
- [ ] Vegan
- [ ] Gluten Free
- [ ] Dairy Free

Likes

Dislikes

Date	Food Served

Guest Name:

Dietary Requirements

☐ Allergies
☐ Vegetarian
☐ Vegan
☐ Gluten Free
☐ Dairy Free

Likes

Dislikes

Date | Food Served

Guest Name:

Dietary Requirements

☐ Allergies
☐ Vegetarian
☐ Vegan
☐ Gluten Free
☐ Dairy Free

Likes

Dislikes

Date | Food Served

Recipe Log

Recipe Log . . .

Title	Page

Title	Page

Recipes

Recipe: ....

☐ Starter   ☐ Main   ☐ Dessert   ☐ Side   ☐ Vegetarian
☐ Vegan

Serves: ....

☐ Gluten Free

Prep time: ....

☐ Dairy Free

Cook time: ....

Ingredients

....
....
....
....
....
....
....

Method or Where To Find The Recipe

....
....
....
....
....
....
....
....
....
....
....

Recipe:

- [ ] Starter - [ ] Main - [ ] Dessert - [ ] Side   - [ ] Vegetarian
- [ ] Vegan
- [ ] Gluten Free
- [ ] Dairy Free

Serves:

Prep time:

Cook time:

Ingredients

Method or Where To Find The Recipe

Recipe:

☐ Starter ☐ Main ☐ Dessert ☐ Side   ☐ Vegetarian
☐ Vegan
☐ Gluten Free
☐ Dairy Free

Serves:

Prep time:

Cook time:

Ingredients

Method or Where To Find The Recipe

Recipe:

☐ Starter ☐ Main ☐ Dessert ☐ Side

☐ Vegetarian
☐ Vegan
☐ Gluten Free
☐ Dairy Free

Serves:

Prep time:

Cook time:

Ingredients

Method or Where To Find The Recipe

Recipe:

- [ ] Starter   - [ ] Main   - [ ] Dessert   - [ ] Side   - [ ] Vegetarian
- [ ] Vegan
- [ ] Gluten Free
- [ ] Dairy Free

Serves:

Prep time:

Cook time:

Ingredients

Method or Where To Find The Recipe

Recipe: ....

☐ Starter ☐ Main ☐ Dessert ☐ Side   ☐ Vegetarian
Serves: .... ☐ Vegan
Prep time: .... ☐ Gluten Free
Cook time: .... ☐ Dairy Free

Ingredients

....
....
....
....
....
....
....

Method or Where To Find The Recipe

....
....
....
....
....
....
....
....
....
....
....
....

Recipe: ....

☐ Starter ☐ Main ☐ Dessert ☐ Side   ☐ Vegetarian
Serves: ....   ☐ Vegan
Prep time: ....   ☐ Gluten Free
Cook time: ....   ☐ Dairy Free

Ingredients

.... | ....
.... | ....
.... | ....
.... | ....
.... | ....
.... | ....
.... | ....

Method or Where To Find The Recipe

....
....
....
....
....
....
....
....
....
....
....
....

Recipe:

☐ Starter ☐ Main ☐ Dessert ☐ Side ☐ Vegetarian
☐ Vegan
☐ Gluten Free
☐ Dairy Free

Serves:

Prep time:

Cook time:

Ingredients

Method or Where To Find The Recipe

Recipe:

☐ Starter ☐ Main ☐ Dessert ☐ Side   ☐ Vegetarian
☐ Vegan
Serves: ....   ☐ Gluten Free
Prep time: ....   ☐ Dairy Free
Cook time: ....

Ingredients

....
....
....
....
....
....
....

Method or Where To Find The Recipe

....
....
....
....
....
....
....
....
....
....
....
....

Recipe:

- [ ] Starter - [ ] Main - [ ] Dessert - [ ] Side - [ ] Vegetarian
- [ ] Vegan
- [ ] Gluten Free
- [ ] Dairy Free

Serves:

Prep time:

Cook time:

Ingredients

Method or Where To Find The Recipe

Recipe:

- [ ] Starter [ ] Main [ ] Dessert [ ] Side
- [ ] Vegetarian
- [ ] Vegan
- [ ] Gluten Free
- [ ] Dairy Free

Serves:

Prep time:

Cook time:

Ingredients

Method or Where To Find The Recipe

Recipe:

- [ ] Starter [ ] Main [ ] Dessert [ ] Side

Serves:...

Prep time:.......................................

Cook time:......................................

- [ ] Vegetarian
- [ ] Vegan
- [ ] Gluten Free
- [ ] Dairy Free

Ingredients

Method or Where To Find The Recipe

Recipe:

- [ ] Starter [ ] Main [ ] Dessert [ ] Side
- [ ] Vegetarian
- [ ] Vegan
- [ ] Gluten Free
- [ ] Dairy Free

Serves:

Prep time:

Cook time:

Ingredients

Method or Where To Find The Recipe

Recipe:

☐ Starter ☐ Main ☐ Dessert ☐ Side ☐ Vegetarian

Serves: .... ☐ Vegan

Prep time: .... ☐ Gluten Free

Cook time: .... ☐ Dairy Free

Ingredients

Method or Where To Find The Recipe

Recipe:

☐ Starter ☐ Main ☐ Dessert ☐ Side   ☐ Vegetarian
☐ Vegan
Serves:
☐ Gluten Free
Prep time:
☐ Dairy Free
Cook time:

Ingredients

Method or Where To Find The Recipe

Recipe: ....

- [ ] Starter [ ] Main [ ] Dessert [ ] Side [ ] Vegetarian
- [ ] Vegan
- [ ] Gluten Free
- [ ] Dairy Free

Serves: ....

Prep time: ....

Cook time: ....

Ingredients

Method or Where To Find The Recipe

Recipe:

- [ ] Starter [ ] Main [ ] Dessert [ ] Side
- [ ] Vegetarian
- [ ] Vegan
- [ ] Gluten Free
- [ ] Dairy Free

Serves:

Prep time:

Cook time:

Ingredients

Method or Where To Find The Recipe

Recipe: ....

☐ Starter ☐ Main ☐ Dessert ☐ Side ☐ Vegetarian
☐ Vegan
Serves: ....
☐ Gluten Free
Prep time: ....
☐ Dairy Free
Cook time: ....

Ingredients

....	....
....	....
....	....
....	....
....	....
....	....

Method or Where To Find The Recipe

....
....
....
....
....
....
....
....
....
....
....
....

Recipe: ....

☐ Starter   ☐ Main   ☐ Dessert   ☐ Side   ☐ Vegetarian

Serves: ....   ☐ Vegan

Prep time: ....   ☐ Gluten Free

Cook time: ....   ☐ Dairy Free

Ingredients

....
....
....
....
....
....
....

Method or Where To Find The Recipe

....
....
....
....
....
....
....
....
....
....
....
....

Recipe:

☐ Starter ☐ Main ☐ Dessert ☐ Side   ☐ Vegetarian

Serves: ....   ☐ Vegan

Prep time: ....   ☐ Gluten Free

Cook time: ....   ☐ Dairy Free

Ingredients

....	....
....	....
....	....
....	....
....	....
....	....

Method or Where To Find The Recipe

Recipe:

- [ ] Starter [ ] Main [ ] Dessert [ ] Side
- [ ] Vegetarian
- [ ] Vegan
- [ ] Gluten Free
- [ ] Dairy Free

Serves: ....

Prep time: ....

Cook time: ....

Ingredients

Method or Where To Find The Recipe

Recipe: ....

- [ ] Starter - [ ] Main - [ ] Dessert - [ ] Side - [ ] Vegetarian
- [ ] Vegan
- [ ] Gluten Free
- [ ] Dairy Free

Serves: ....

Prep time: ....

Cook time: ....

Ingredients

....
....
....
....
....
....
....

Method or Where To Find The Recipe

....
....
....
....
....
....
....
....
....
....
....
....
....

Recipe:

☐ Starter ☐ Main ☐ Dessert ☐ Side ☐ Vegetarian
☐ Vegan
Serves:
☐ Gluten Free
Prep time:
☐ Dairy Free
Cook time:

Ingredients

Method or Where To Find The Recipe

Recipe:

☐ Starter ☐ Main ☐ Dessert ☐ Side   ☐ Vegetarian

Serves: ....   ☐ Vegan

Prep time: ....   ☐ Gluten Free

Cook time: ....   ☐ Dairy Free

Ingredients

Method or Where To Find The Recipe

Recipe:

- [ ] Starter [ ] Main [ ] Dessert [ ] Side
- [ ] Vegetarian
- [ ] Vegan
- [ ] Gluten Free
- [ ] Dairy Free

Serves:

Prep time:

Cook time:

Ingredients

Method or Where To Find The Recipe

Recipe:

- [ ] Starter [ ] Main [ ] Dessert [ ] Side
- [ ] Vegetarian
- [ ] Vegan
- [ ] Gluten Free
- [ ] Dairy Free

Serves:

Prep time:

Cook time:

Ingredients

Method or Where To Find The Recipe

Recipe:

- [ ] Starter - [ ] Main - [ ] Dessert - [ ] Side - [ ] Vegetarian
- [ ] Vegan
- [ ] Gluten Free
- [ ] Dairy Free

Serves: ....

Prep time: ....

Cook time: ....

Ingredients

....
....
....
....
....
....
....

Method or Where To Find The Recipe

....
....
....
....
....
....
....
....
....
....
....

Recipe:

☐ Starter ☐ Main ☐ Dessert ☐ Side ☐ Vegetarian
☐ Vegan
Serves:
☐ Gluten Free
Prep time:
☐ Dairy Free
Cook time:

Ingredients

Method or Where To Find The Recipe

Recipe: ....

- [ ] Starter [ ] Main [ ] Dessert [ ] Side   [ ] Vegetarian
- [ ] Vegan
- [ ] Gluten Free
- [ ] Dairy Free

Serves: ....

Prep time: ....

Cook time: ....

Ingredients

....
....
....
....
....
....
....

Method or Where To Find The Recipe

....

....

....

....

....

....

....

....

....

....

Recipe:

- [ ] Starter [ ] Main [ ] Dessert [ ] Side
- [ ] Vegetarian
- [ ] Vegan
- [ ] Gluten Free
- [ ] Dairy Free

Serves:

Prep time:

Cook time:

Ingredients

Method or Where To Find The Recipe

Recipe: ....

☐ Starter ☐ Main ☐ Dessert ☐ Side   ☐ Vegetarian

Serves: ....   ☐ Vegan

Prep time: ....   ☐ Gluten Free

Cook time: ....   ☐ Dairy Free

Ingredients

....	....
....	....
....	....
....	....
....	....
....	....
....	....
....	....

Method or Where To Find The Recipe

....
....
....
....
....
....
....
....
....
....
....
....

Recipe:

☐ Starter ☐ Main ☐ Dessert ☐ Side   ☐ Vegetarian
☐ Vegan
Serves: ....
☐ Gluten Free
Prep time: ....
☐ Dairy Free
Cook time: ....

Ingredients

....
....
....
....
....
....
....

Method or Where To Find The Recipe

....
....
....
....
....
....
....
....
....
....
....
....

Kitchen Measurements

Volume Conversion

Measure	UK	US
Teaspoon	5 ml	5 ml
Tablespoon	15 ml	15 ml
fl oz	28 ml	28 ml
1 Cup / 8 fl oz	237 ml	237 ml
2 Cups / Pint	474 ml	474 ml
4 Cups ¾ Quart	946 ml	946 ml
16 Cups / Gallon	3.8 L	3.8 L

Measure	Australia
Teaspoon	5 ml
Tablespoon	20 ml
½ Cup	125 ml
1 Cup	250 ml
1 ½ Cups	375 ml
2 Cups	500 ml
5 Cups	1.25 L

Weight Conversion

ounces	grams
½ oz	10 g
¾ oz	20 g
1 oz	25 g
1½ oz	40 g
2 oz	50 g
2½ oz	60 g
3 oz	75 g
4 oz	110 g
4½ oz	125 g
5 oz	150 g
6 oz	175 g
7 oz	200 g
8 oz	225 g
9 oz	250 g
10 oz	275 g
12 oz	350 g
1 lb	450 g

Oven Temperature Conversion

GAS	°F	°C	FAN °C
1	275	140	120
2	300	150	130
3	325	170	150
4	350	180	160
5	375	190	170
6	400	200	180
7	425	220	200
8	450	230	210
9	475	240	220

Reflections

Memorable Moments . . .

Things That Went Wrong...

Laugh Out Loud Moments . . .

Recipes I Must Make Again . . .

Recipes I Must Never Make Again . . .

Ideas I've Seen That I'd Like To Try...

FOOD FOR FRIENDS

Let's Get Organised collection, first published by **FROM YOU TO ME LTD** in September 2024

For a full range of all our titles where gifts can also be personalised, please visit

WWW.FROMYOUTOME.COM

FROM YOU TO ME are committed to a sustainable future for our business, our customers and our planet. This book is printed and bound in China on FSC® certified paper.

All rights reserved. No part of this publication may be reproduced, stored in a retrieval system, or transmitted in any form or by any means electronic, mechanical, photocopying, recording, or otherwise, without the prior written permission of the copyright owner who can be contacted via the publisher at the above website address.

1 3 5 7 9 11 13 15 14 12 10 8 6 4 2

Copyright © 2024 **FROM YOU TO ME LTD**

ISBN 978-1-907048-80-7

FROM YOU TO ME LTD, STUDIO 100, THE OLD LEATHER FACTORY
GLOVE FACTORY STUDIOS, HOLT, WILTSHIRE, BA14 6RJ